Before Knossos…

Arthur Evans's Travels

in the Balkans and Crete

FRONTISPIECE: **Arthur Evans** *c.* 1878.
(From Joan Evans, *Time and Chance* **(1943) pl. p.165)**

Before Knossos . . .

Arthur Evans's travels

in the Balkans and Crete

Ann Brown

University of Oxford
Ashmolean Museum
Oxford
1993

British Library cataloguing-in-publication data:
A catalogue record of this book is available from the British Library

ISBN1 85444 0292 paperback
ISBN1 85444 0306 hardback

Designed by Keith Bennett

Printed and bound in Great Britain by Cheney & Sons Ltd., Banbury, 1993

Contents

Acknowledgements ———— 6

Chronology ———— 6

Introduction ———— 9

Early Years ———— 11

Balkan Correspondent ———— 19

Ashmole's Keeper ———— 29

The Cretan Thread ———— 35

Cretan Politics ———— 36

The first visit to Crete ———— 37

'A Mycenaean Military Way' ———— 54

Explorations in Eastern Crete ———— 64

North Africa ———— 75

News from Crete ———— 76

Letters from Crete ———— 76

The year before Knossos ———— 80

Epilogue ———— 84

Select Bibliography ———— 87

Maps ———— 89

Acknowledgements

I would like to thank Vasso Fotou and Stephen Townsend, both of whom explored and photographed some of the more inaccessible sites visited by Evans. The former also helped me in preparing the text. Volunteers in the Department of Antiquities, Steven Thompson, Claudia Woods and most especially Helen Kempshall, have helped in various ways and I am very grateful to them. Keith Bennett has designed the book and I deeply appreciate his unfailing help in its preparation. Finally I would like to thank the Keeper of the Department of Antiquities, Dr Roger Moorey for his encouragement and patience.

The Arthur Evans Will Trust has kindly allowed me to quote from Evans's Notebooks; other original material is illustrated and quoted through the generosity of Mr Arthur Evans, and the Pitt Rivers Museum, University of Oxford. I should also like to thank Dr Caroline Barron. The sources of the illustrations are acknowledged in the plate captions. Other photographs have been taken in the Ashmolean Museum's studio by Nick Pollard.

Ann Brown

Chronology

Early Minoan	*c. 3650—2160*
Middle Minoan	*c. 2160—1600*
Late Minoan	*c. 1600—1070*

The dates in the above table are B.C.
Based on P. Warren and V. Hankey, Aegean Bronze Age Chronology *(1989)*

Colour pl. A   Tulip, Anemone, Iris, Cyclamen, Arum Lily and Peony
(Photographs by Author).

Introduction

During the Ashmolean Museum's Tercentenary celebrations in 1983 the Museum published *Arthur Evans and the Palace of Minos*; in this book I illustrated the excavations at Knossos, which began in 1900 and made Evans enduringly renowned. The present booklet covers the main events of Evans's life, particularly his travels, before he began work at Knossos.

Its appearance marks the centenary of the transfer, organised by Evans in 1894, of the Ashmolean Museum's collections from their original home in Broad Street, now the Museum of the History of Science, to the recently extended University Galleries in Beaumont Street. It was this achievement that entitles him to be known as the 'second founder' of the Ashmolean Museum.

Already before 1894 Evans had made a name for himself as a journalist reporting on the Balkans. An enthusiastic traveller, he kept diaries, detailing his Balkan journeys, and later Cretan travels, and he filled sketchbooks with drawings of people, objects and landscapes.

In the Spring of 1894 Evans paid his first visit to Crete and was enchanted. During his annual travels in the island from 1894 to 1899 (excepting 1897) he was fascinated, not only by the grandeur of the Cretan landscape and its wild flowers (colour pl. A), but above all by the remains of its prehistoric culture, which he was to call 'Minoan'. Many of the ancient sites he visited have still not been excavated, and his sketches shed new light on some already well-known. This book briefly describes a selection of such sites; a more detailed work, including a transcription of Evans's Cretan travel diaries, is in preparation.

Arthur Evans was a prolific writer—books, articles, letters and sketch-filled diaries provide extensive evidence for his experiences, discoveries and the changes he witnessed. The primary source materials used in this booklet are kept in the School of Slavonic and East European Studies, University of London; the Pitt Rivers Museum, Oxford; and the Ashmolean Museum and Library, Oxford.

Fig. 1 John Evans (1823—1908) *c.* 1865.

Arthur John Evans's interests in archaeology and travel date back to childhood. He was born in 1851 at the Red House, Nash Mills, Hertfordshire the eldest child of John Evans (fig. 1), an eminent archaeologist, numismatist, geologist, and collector of coins and antiquities. Arthur grew up under the shadow of his father, 'Little Evans—son of John Evans the Great' (fig. 2), with all the advantages and disadvantages that this implied. His mother, Harriet, was the daughter of John Dickinson, a wealthy paper manufacturer, who made John Evans his partner. In spite of his mother's death when he was only six years old, Arthur had a happy childhood. He became extremely fond of his stepmother Fanny, and wrote many letters to her from Callipers, his preparatory school, and later from Harrow School. These reveal that he was already interested in collecting objects (fig. 3). He enjoyed arranging his father's collections of bronze and stone weapons and tools, and when he was a little older he listened to the discussions of his father's friends, the most forward-looking archaeologists and scientists of the day. In 1859 Darwin, who was an acquaintance of John Evans, published On the Origin of Species; and a friend, Augustus Lane Fox (who later took the name Pitt-Rivers), put forward the idea of the *Evolution of Culture*, in which the typological study of objects was set out. Other friends who shared his father's interests included Charles Roach Smith, Sir John Lubbock and Augustus Franks of the British Museum.

When he was only nine years old Arthur went on an expedition to Dunwich in Suffolk, where a village had been lost to the sea, to search for mediaeval pottery. Later he accompanied his father to France and saw man-made tools in juxtaposition with fossils in the Somme gravel pits, the significance of which John Evans had been the first in Britain to appreciate. Arthur's interest in archaeology grew, and in 1868 he accompanied his father to Ipswich to the meeting of the British Association for the Advancement of Science. His academic achievements at school were not brilliant, although he won prizes for English poems and Greek epigrams. He failed to get into the college of his choice at Oxford, but his housemaster at Harrow, F. Rendall wrote to the Principal of Brasenose College, Oxford: 'Dear Sir, I write to let you know that my pupil A.J. Evans, now a candidate for admission at your college, is a monitor at Harrow

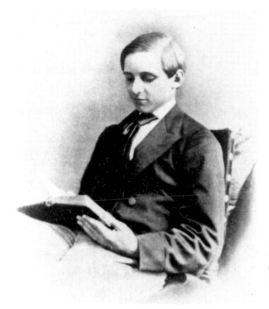

Fig. 2 Arthur John Evans (1851—1941) *c.* 1867. (From, Joan Evans, *Time and Chance* (1943), pl. p. 164).

Harrow on the hill

March 12 1868

My dear Mamma

I am so glad that Norman has found the flints at last, he must be pleased. I suppose Pa has just come back from Canterbury. if so will you ask him if he thinks this buckle to be old from the picture. I picked it up the other day when I went to see a British Earthwork, near Pinner station. the Earthwork was very large with the moat full of water & ~~feet~~ deep in some places, & it was so long that although I walked along it for ever such a way I couldn't find a beginning or an End. this buckle I found in the only piece of ploughed field along the whole way & it is of a kind of greenish colour except the spike which is iron. but I couldn't find any arrowheads not even a scraper, or flake was to be seen. The other day I & some other boys in this house were invited to Breakfast by Mrs Butler & Dr Butler, who were very kind & amusing. I send my love to all & am

Your affec son

Arthur.

P.S. all right & I suppose you will come next Wednesday as you said. Has Mr Rendall sent you any invitation yet.

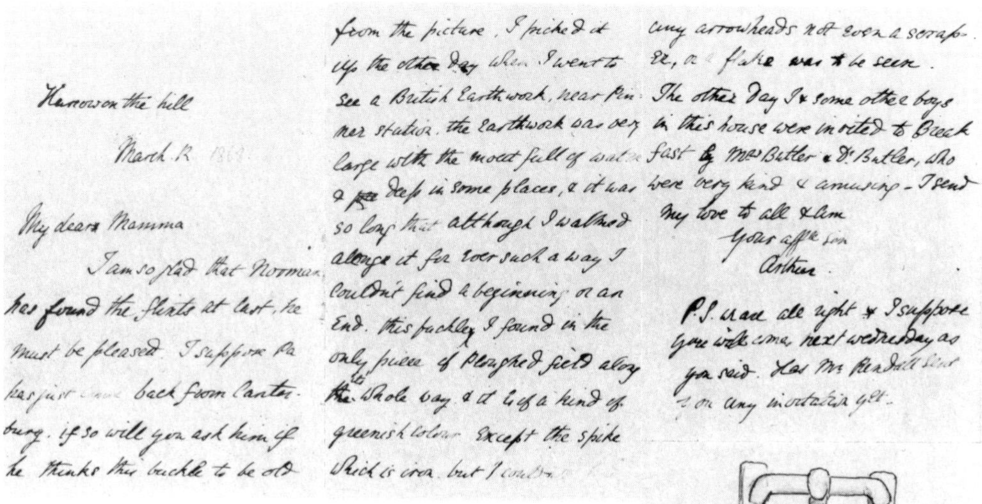

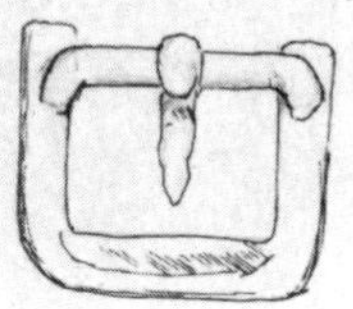

Fig. 3 Letter from Arthur Evans to his Stepmother Fanny, written 12th March, 1868, from Harrow School. (Ashmolean Museum).

School, of unblemished moral character. You will find him a boy of powerful original mind I think, if any questions in your matriculation examination should take him off the beaten track.' He was accepted by Brasenose College, where he read Modern History. In his final examination he broke down when questioned in his viva, but in spite of this and answering no question on a period later than the twelfth century A.D., he was awarded a first class honours degree (fig. 4).

Fig. 4   Degree Certificate, 1874, signed by the Regius Professor of Modern History, W. Stubbs; and the History Examiners G.W. Kitchen, and J.R. Green. (Ashmolean Museum).

During his undergraduate days Arthur used his vacations to travel abroad, visiting little known places. In 1871 he and his brother Lewis visited Hallstatt in Austria, then Carinthia and Carniola (Slovenia), stayed at Agram (Croatia, modern Zagreb) and Sizsek, whence they journeyed seven hours to Kostainica, where Arthur met Turks for the first time. He was fascinated and bought a set of Turkish clothes complete with fez. He admired the Turks, but grew to hate their oppressive rule. The following year he went to eastern Europe with his brother Norman, who was still at Harrow School. They reached Romania, travelling without passports, which presented considerable difficulties. The two boys often slept rough, and had to slip through trees, revolvers at the ready, to avoid the border guards. Arthur published a graphic account of their adventures in *Fraser's Magazine* (May 1873). He noted everything: the flowers and butterflies in the Carpathian mountains, the people and their costumes; he wrote of the men in sheepskin mantles and great shaggy caps, describing how, when it was not raining, they discarded these and 'walk about in the full glory of flowing white trousers and tunic, and a broad leathern dagger-belt round their waist indented with strange spiral decorations, and curiously reminding one of the bronze belts discovered in the pre-historic cemetery at Hallstadt.' Already Evans was drawing comparisons between ancient and modern artefacts and establishing links between different areas.

From August to October 1873, Evans went north (map 1), travelling by rickety cart, foot and boat, visiting Sweden, 'land of cream, wild strawberries, blue eyes and flaxen hair,' and out-of-the-way places in Finland. He hired a Lapp guide called Johanninpoika Marataja (fig. 5), 'Alias "The Grand Irreclaimable Savage"', and later a reindeer to carry the baggage (fig. 6). He visited fishing villages around the lakes (figs. 7—8), and was told of a sacred grotto on the island

Fig. 5 'Our Lapp guide Johanninpoika Marataja—on the shore of Lake Inare' Wearing a 'leather belt, coarse sackcloth tunic but with a high collar of divers colours, which is the distinguishing feature of the Lapp tunic—his legs closely sheathed in the same ragged sacking.' Drawing by Evans. (Pitt Rivers Museum).

Fig. 6 'Our Reindeer. Near Armonjarvi. Tornea, Lappmark, Finland.' Unfortunately 'the saddle was not good we couldn't balance the knapsacks properly and the reindeer kept twisting about and butting the Lapp who led him... we had to give him up as a bad job, and send him home by his driver.' Drawing by Evans. (Pitt Rivers Museum).

Fig. 7 'Fisher Lapp (little girl). Coast of Lake Inare...There is a little girl of 3 in a Lapp cap and blue tunic with the usual blue stripes about it.' Drawing by Evans. (Pitt Rivers Museum).

of Ukonsaari, on Lake Inare (fig. 9). The island, he noted, 'seen from its side looks rather like a great tortoise swimming with a head and tail at its ends'. He carried out a small, 'very superficial' excavation in the cave, and found a silver 'ear-ring' (fig. 10) and, outside the cave, a half-circle of reindeer antlers, 'very old and somewhat disturbed'. When it was time to return to Oxford Evans crossed the wilds of Finland and reached Sweden, but found the region tame, lacking any spice of danger and having little of archaeological interest. He returned home wearing a reindeer skin coat, the smell of which was so offensive to his stepmother that she wrote: 'I can't think how he could bear himself'.

Adventure gave way to study: in 1875 Arthur went to Göttingen University. He made good use of the library, but found lectures unhelpful and his lodgings (fig. 11) rather uncomfortable, partly because he was provided with a duvet, which he dubbed a 'suffocator'.

15

Fig. 8 Sheds for nets, winter stores; for drying fish and curing skins. Dwelling house of wood, hides, turf and thatch. Settlement on Lake Hammasjayri. Drawing by Evans. (Pitt Rivers Museum).

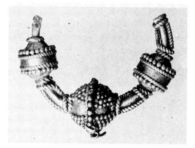

Fig. 9 Ukonsaari, sacred to the God of Thunder, Ukon. 'Half way up is the grotto used by the Lapps as an offering-place, and where the silver ear-ring of Arabian workmanship was found by us.' Drawing by Evans. (Pitt Rivers Museum).

Fig. 10 'Ear-ring'. Date 12th century A.D., Ashmolean no. 1919.60, Diam. of bow 0.038

Fig. 11 Göttingen. 'Front view of my house. The two upper windows are mine.' Drawing by Evans. (Ashmolean Museum).

On his way to Göttingen he carried out an illicit excavation at a Roman cemetery near Trier, finding lamps and brooches (fig. 12). Although pursuing his academic interests, Evans was perhaps more interested in the people he met, their way of life and their political aspirations. This was particularly true of his travels in the Balkans.

Leaving Göttingen he was joined by his brother Lewis at Agram, where they visited the 'crockery market to study crocks' (fig. 13), comparing modern

Fig. 12 (below) **Roman lamps and brooch inlaid with** *niello,* **excavated by Evans at Trier. Ashmolean nos. R.309, 312; 1927.204**

Fig. 13 (left) **Agram. 'Went into Crockery market to study crocks. The chief forms are a wine, beer or water jug—called Peha.' Drawing by Evans.** (Ashmolean Museum).

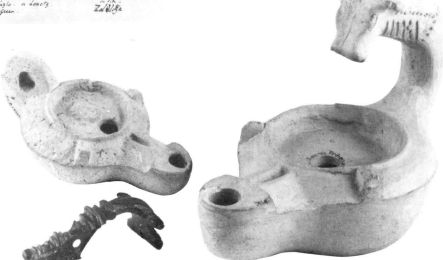

Croat vessels with Roman vases. They planned to visit the Ottoman provinces of Bosnia and Herzegovina (map 2), which had been placed under martial law. This time Evans had learnt his lesson and they travelled with passes. In spite of this they were taken for Russian spies and briefly imprisoned in Brood. Evans was to remember the 'wretched cell some seven feet by ten' when, over twenty years later, his muleteer was incarcerated in a police cell in Crete.

Eventually they reached the important town of Tesanj where Evans sketched the scene in a Turkish cafe (fig. 14). Many of his drawings reflect an interest in costume. His own costume caused consternation: 'The combined effect of an Indian helmet and Norfolk coatee is in these parts quite appalling.'

Fig. 14 'Turkish Cafe, Tesanj.' Drawing by Evans. (Pitt Rivers Museum).

Approaching the Bosnian capital of Sarajevo they learned that insurrection was spreading throughout the area as Christian peasants were taking up arms and challenging their Bosnian overlords, the Beys, whose forebears had embraced Islam many centuries earlier. Turkish regular soldiers, combined with the irregular followers of the nobles, known as Bashi-Bazouks (Evans was to meet Bashi-Bazouks again in Crete), were unable to crush the revolt, which extended to Herzegovina. Arthur and Lewis spent their last morning in Sarajevo looking for seals and amulets and were successful in acquiring a first century B.C. cornelian seal, engraved with a faun holding an amphora over his shoulder (now in a private collection).

They crossed into Herzegovina and eventually, after many dangerous encounters, reached the capital Mostar. From there they joined a caravan of sixty horsemen as far as the town of Metković, near the Dalmatian frontier, where they hired a 'flat beetle-like craft'. After at length reaching Ragusa (Dubrovnik), Evans looked for Roman sculpture in the old town—losing his heart to the city, which he was later to make his home. On his return to Oxford, Evans found life extremely dull, but re-lived his travels when writing *Through Bosnia and the Herzegovina on foot during the Insurrection, August and September 1875*. The book, published in 1876, was reviewed in the *Manchester Guardian*: 'This is a most opportune contribution to the geography, customs, and history of a country which has suddenly emerged from the dimmest obscurity into the full glare of European observation...' The book was a great success, extensively quoted in Parliament and indeed all over the country; a second edition appeared the following year.

Balkan Correspondent

Evans applied unsuccessfully for college fellowships which would have enabled him to pursue an academic career in Oxford. Such an appointment, with its enclosed life and endless committee meetings, would probably have frustrated such a mercurial traveller. Luckily, C.P. Scott, editor of the *Manchester Guardian* offered him the post of Balkans correspondent. Before taking the appointment he sought the advice of *The Times* Balkan correspondent, W.J. Stillman. This connection was to stand him in good stead. Stillman had been American consul in Crete during the horrific siege of the Christians by the Turks at the Monastery of Arkadi in 1866 (fig. 15), and was to return to Crete later.

Evans set out for the Balkans in 1877, and visited the troubled regions, often at great personal danger. Many of his reports to the *Manchester Guardian* were later published as *Illyrian Letters*. They give eyewitness accounts of the sufferings of the Christian peasants at the hands of the Turks, and describe a visit to the Moslem rulers, who believed Evans to be an ambassador from the Great Powers. Evans did not see the uprisings as part of the wider Eastern Question. He was extremely critical of the British government and its Consul, who appeared to believe the Turkish version of events. His anti-Turkish views reflected those of Gladstone who, although no longer in power, was still active in politics. British foreign policy was being dictated by the fear that the disintegration of the Ottoman Empire would lead to the expansion of Russian influence.

Fig. 15   The siege of the Monastery of Arkadi 1866. (From *Illustrated London News*, Nov. 1866).

Concurrently with his activities as a journalist, Evans was able to pursue his archaeological interests. He collected a considerable number of seals (fig. 16) and also bought a small 'pendant', which probably once decorated an earring (colour pl. B). He started excavating a large barrow at Canali, but his work was interrupted when war broke out between the Turks and Montenegrins. Evans left to report from Cettinje, but was able to return and continue the excavation later (fig. 17).

Fig. 16 Cornelian ringstone and impression, bust of a youth. From Narona. Late 2nd/early 1st century B.C. Ashmolean no. 1941.283 (Photograph by R. Wilkins).

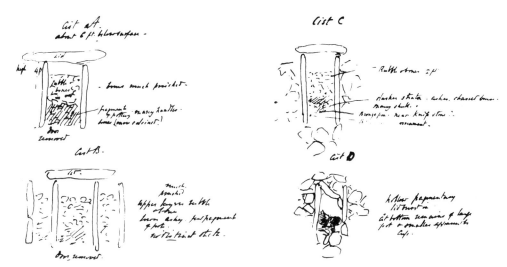

Fig. 17 'Excavation at Canali.' Drawing by Evans. (Ashmolean Museum).

21

He found pins and spirals of bronze and a stone knife; he gave a small stone axe from the site (colour pl. B) to his father. The objects he found led him to date the barrow to the Early Bronze Age. Heading notes on the excavation, 'Cannibal Canali', he wrote: 'It appears they burnt the chieftain and then slew victims including (Cist C) enceinte woman, but having a frugal mind they ate them first, all bones shaftbones ie. had lost their cancellous tissue and had their ends broken or bitten off and some showed tooth-marks... I suppose in those days eating yr deceased friend was as sacred a duty as closing his eyes at a later period.'

One of the most attractive objects he acquired on his travels was a marble head of Hermes from the Roman colony of Narona, part of a 2nd century B.C. Roman sarcophagus (fig. 18). He was said to have obtained it in

Fig. 18   Marble head of Hermes, from a Roman sarcophagus. 2nd century B.C. Given by Dame Joan Evans. Ashmolean no. 1974.438

Colour pl. B   Arkadi Monastery, watercolour by Edward Lear, from a sketch dated 1864. (Ashmolean Museum).

Pendant, probably from an earring. From Risano. *c.* A.D. 900, Diam.0.018. Ashmolean no. M.190.

Stone axe said to come from Cilipi, Canali. Early Bronze Age. Ht.0.042. Ashmolean no. 1927.5935.

DIAGRAMMATIC MAP OF SLAV TERRITORIES EAST OF THE ADRIATIC
BY ARTHUR EVANS, (ISSUED FOR THE BALKAN COMMITTEE)

Colour pl. C   Map prepared by Evans for the Balkan Committee 1913.
(Ashmolean Museum).

24

exchange for a fine top hat made by Locks, the St. James' Street hatter. The head travelled back to England in the empty hat box.

The largely successful 1875 uprising against the Turks in Bosnia encouraged the Bulgars to rise in 1876, aided by the Serbs. The Turks retaliated viciously and the Russians were drawn into the conflict. By January 1878 Russian forces were outside the gates of Constantinople. Turkey was forced to accept harsh terms, and Bosnia and Herzegovina were placed under the protection of the Austro-Hungarian Empire: one master had been replaced by another.

Fig. 19   Wedding photograph taken outside Somerleaze.
Standing: **Florence Freeman, Harriet Evans, Norman Evans, Helen Freeman, Mr Evans, Alice Evans, Mrs Evans, Lewis Evans, Kate Freeman, Harold Freeman.**
Sitting: **Edgar Freeman, Mr Freeman, Margaret, Arthur, Mrs Freeman, Edward Manson.**
(Ashmolean Museum).

Meanwhile the previous year, 1877, Evans had met Augustus Freeman, the historian who later became Regius Professor of Modern History at Oxford. Freeman was travelling with two of his daughters, who were aiding Miss Irby, a redoubtable English lady working for the Bosnian refugees. They were pleased to meet Evans, who had already met Miss Irby in 1875 and become secretary to the Refugee Relief Fund. Freeman approved Evans's Liberal views and wrote that he 'was mightily taken with the lad'.

In September 1878 Arthur Evans married Freeman's eldest daughter, Margaret. The ceremony took place in Wookey Parish Church and was conducted by the Bishop of Bath and Wells. The wedding photograph was taken outside the Freemans' home, Somerleaze, near Wookey (fig. 19). The couple returned to Ragusa where they lived at Casa San Lazzaro. The house overlooking the sea (fig. 20) was soon made attractive by Margaret and the garden was planted with vines, figs, olives and many flowers. It later became the taverna of the Hotel Excelsior. From his base at Ragusa Evans continued his journalistic career, visiting Herzegovina, from where his reports were viewed with suspicion by the Austrians. Eventually he was accused of spying and in 1882 was given three days notice to quit the country. But at the quay he was met by gendarmes and soldiers with fixed bayonets, arrested, imprisoned, and charged with high treason (fig. 21). Although freed after six weeks (fig. 22), he was banished from the Austro-Hungarian Empire.

Fig. 20   Casa San Lazzaro, Ragusa. (Ashmolean Museum).

MARCH 9, 1882.

THE RISING IN THE EAST.

THE ARREST OF AN ENGLISH CORRESPONDENT.

(BY SUBMARINE TELEGRAPH.)
(FROM OUR OWN CORRESPONDENT.)
VIENNA, WEDNESDAY NIGHT.

Yesterday at midday Mr. Evans and his wife drove to Gravosa. When they alighted from their carriage at the landing place to go on board the San Carlo, bound for Cattaro, they were stopped by the gendarmes, arrested, and taken to the barracks. Possibly the Austrian authorities will justify this step by the exceptional law promulgated on the 6th for the Cattaro, Ragusa, and Metkovic districts, which suspends for the time the freedom and protection granted to all subjects, and authorises the Government to take extraordinary measures when necessary. Mr. Evans's arrest is much commented upon here. Mr. Evans came to Austria about three years ago, and leased a country house near Ragusa, which he furnished in English style. In the fulfilment of his journalistic duties he continually passed between Northern Dalmatia and the newly-acquired provinces. The Government, for reasons best known to itself, seems to have come to the conclusion that he was a dangerous agitator, and apparently have now treated him as such. People here will indeed gravely tell you that he has everywhere encouraged opposition to the army law. It is to be assumed that before arresting him the Government had some positive facts to go by, but these are not known. Mr. Evans cannot be brought before a military court, because his offences, whatever they may be, were committed before the promulgation of the exceptional law in Dalmatia. He was oftentimes spoken of by those who ought to have known better as "Lord Evans." His wife assists him in his literary pursuits.

FRIDAY, APRIL 28, 1882.

THE RELEASE OF MR. EVANS.

(FROM A CORRESPONDENT.)
VIENNA TUESDAY EVENING.

The *Politische Correspondenz*, a Government organ, publishes the following note on the case of Mr. Evans:— "Mr. Evans's attitude, his frequent excursions into Herzegovina, and his intercourse with the chiefs of the insurrectionary movement, were the cause of his expulsion from Austrian territory. Subsequently an inquiry instituted against the Austrian subjects Herren Gopevich and Alexis Sevela showed his participation in a conspiracy against Austria, and this led to his arrest as he was leaving the country. Inasmuch, however, as it was impossible in the present troublous condition of affairs to prove his culpability by positive evidence of witnesses (this being unobtainable) the Tribunal decided to release him, the condition being that he should leave the country forthwith. The central authorities at Vienna deny that they had any part in the action of the Tribunal, which acted without the least instruction from the authorities, and apart from any influence of the Government organs here."

Fig. 21 (left) **The arrest of Evans.** (*Daily News*, March 9, 1882).

Fig. 22 (above) **The release of Evans.** (*Manchester Guardian*, April 28, 1882).

In spite of this bitter blow, Evans never abandoned his interest in the area. During the Balkan wars (1912—13) his expertise was called on and he drew up a map for the Balkan Committee (colour pl. C), of which he was a longstanding member. During the Great War his house echoed with the games of Serbian boys—refugees from the fighting, who were camping in the grounds. When after the war the allied leaders met to redraw the boundaries of Europe, Evans flew to Paris to represent the interests of the Kingdom of the Serbs, Croats and Slovenes (later known as Yugoslavia). Grateful to Evans for the part he played in liberating the Southern Slavs from the Turks, Yugoslavian representatives were present at his memorial service in 1941.

Evans found life restricted back in England, where he and Margaret rented a house in Broad Street, Oxford. It was not until he visited Crete over a decade later that he was to experience again a sense of excitement and awakened curiosity.

In 1883 Arthur, without employment, spent much time writing about his archaeological discoveries in the Balkans. He made a notable contribution to the archaeology of the region, particularly in tracing the network of Roman roads and identifying Roman cities. He published his findings in two long articles in *Archaeologia* vols. 48 (1884) and 49 (1885).

In the spring of 1883 Arthur and Margaret were able to make a long trip to Greece and the Eastern Balkans. They travelled through Delphi to Arachova, from where they walked some five hours to the Monastery of Hosios Loukas or St. Luke of Stiris (fig. 23). They saw Schliemann's excavations at Orchomenos before finally reaching Athens. Here they visited the Acropolis Museum and marvelled at the brightly painted statues which had been recently excavated.

Fig. 23   The Monastery of Hosios Loukas. Drawing by Evans (Ashmolean Museum).

Margaret complained in her *Diary* that they clambered up to the Acropolis only to find it shut for four days over Easter. She sensibly suggested that they should 'utilize the flag-staff on the acropolis to say if it is closed or not'. In Athens they went to one of Mrs Schliemann's parties and saw the little 'home museum'. Schliemann, whose thoughts had turned to Crete, had written earlier in the year to Photiades Pasha, the Governor, expressing a wish to excavate at Knossos—an objective he was to pursue unsuccessfully until his death in 1891. There is no evidence that Schliemann discussed Crete with Evans and Margaret records only a banal conversation. Arthur and Margaret, anxious to see the source of Schliemann's rich finds, visited Mycenae, marvelling at the Lion Gate, and the towering walls of Tiryns.

Ashmole's Keeper

In June 1884 Evans was appointed Keeper of the Ashmolean. He set out his ambition for the Museum in his inaugural lecture, '*The Ashmolean Museum as a Home of Archaeology in Oxford*'. He planned to make the Museum a centre of excellence, embracing the whole range of European archaeology. The Museum in Broad Street was already overcrowded, its space eroded and used for other purposes. Evans was soon to make important additions to its collections. Travelling with Margaret and his father-in-law, he frequently visited Sicily, where he collected Greek vases in Gela (fig. 24), and on the mainland he acquired terracottas in Taranto (fig. 25). The packing of such fragile objects presented some difficulty and Margaret viewed the problem with dismay; some she wrapped in underwear, others were transported back to Oxford in a picnic basket. Arthur inherited an interest in numismatics from his father and added Sicilian coins (fig. 26) to his already large collection of ancient coins. In spite of his efforts, Evans was unable to persuade the authorities that the natural home for the Bodleian Library's coin collection was the Ashmolean; it was not until 1922 that his plan, suggested in 1884, was realised and the Heberden Coin Room in the Ashmolean was officially opened.

Fig. 26   Coin of Syracuse. Bronze decadrachm, reverse: Head of Arethusa. *c.* 405 B.C. (Heberden Coin Room, Ashmolean Museum).

Fig. 24   Attic red-figure pelike, by the Pan Painter. A youth carrying a couch and table. *c.* 480 B.C. From Gela. Ht.0.284, Ashmolean no. 1890.29

Fig. 25   Terracotta horse's head, from a Sanctuary at Taranto. *c.* 400 B.C. L.0.11, Ashmolean no. 1886.650.

As archaeological interest in the Mediterranean Region and Egypt grew, through excavations by Petrie and others, so Evans was able to collect material and expand the Ashmolean collections. He wooed, with single-minded determination, Charles Drury Edward Fortnum (fig. 27), a collector whose wealth came from the Piccadilly grocery, Fortnum and Mason. Fortnum had already corresponded with John Henry Parker (fig. 28), Evans's predecessor at the Ashmolean. Fortnum and Parker had a vision of a new Ashmolean which would incorporate the University's collection of art and archaeology. Evans embraced and expanded this view. Fortnum had hoped to lend, and ultimately bequeath, his important collection of majolica, ancient and Renaissance bronzes, rings and other objects to the University. But he felt rebuffed by the University authorities, particularly by the Vice-Chancellor, the Reverend Benjamin Jowett, who raised

Fig. 27 **'*L'Amateur chez lui.*' Portrait of Charles Drury Edward Fortnum in his study at Stanmore House, by Charles Alexander.** (Ashmolean Museum).

Fig. 28   John Henry Parker. Keeper of
the Ashmolean Museum 1870—1884.
(Ashmolean Museum).

seemingly spurious objections to his scheme. Evans went into battle on the
Museum's behalf. His sister, Alice, wrote to Margaret: 'You don't expect me to
condole with the Keeper on his prospective difficulties with Jowett? I should
congratulate him on a fight, if not on a "grievance". I can see him snuffing up
the tainted breeze and pawing like a war horse...'

Evans and Fortnum probably exaggerated Jowett's opposition, but Evans
was determined to gain sympathy for his plans within the University, and he
persuaded Fortnum to lend part of his collection, to be shown to a large and
influential University audience in the recently restored Upper Gallery in the
Ashmolean. However, in spite of the support of these newly won allies, it was
not until June 1892 that Fortnum's magnificent collection, together with
funding, was finally accepted. A new museum was planned to house this
collection, the contents of the old Ashmolean and the scattered archaeological

collections belonging to the University. The new extension, behind the University Galleries in Beaumont Street, was completed in 1894, and from August to November the objects were carried to their present home, the most precious of them in hand-carts. At the same time Evans moved into Youlbury, the grandiose house that he had built for himself and Margaret on Boar's Hill, near Oxford (fig. 29). This move must have been a sad occasion; Margaret, who had been his companion and helper for fifteen years, had died the previous year. Although outwardly stoical Arthur was deeply affected by her death and he revealed some of his feelings in a short sentimental poem (fig. 30). The moves of the Autumn of 1894 however were preceded by Evans's first visit to Crete which was to change his whole life.

Fig. 29 Youlbury, Boar's Hill, Oxford. Photographed shortly before demolition in 1951. (Ashmolean Museum).

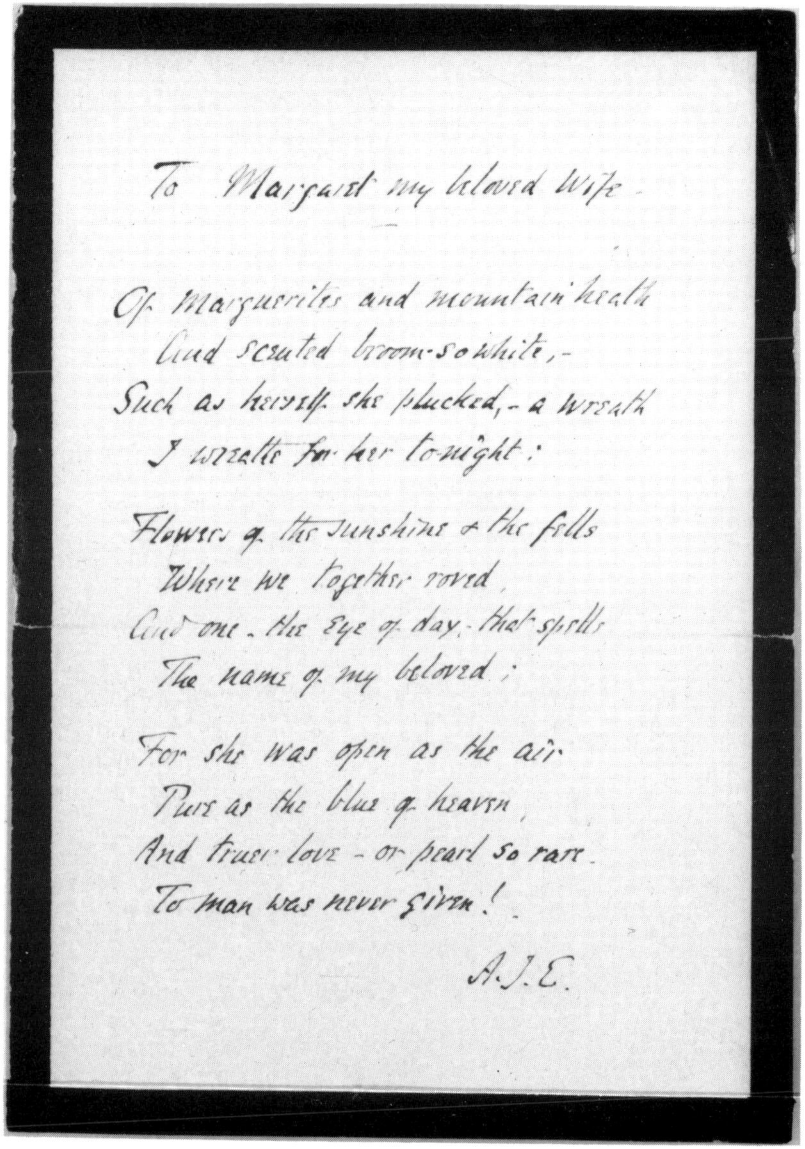

To Margaret my beloved Wife —

Of marguerites and mountain heath
And scented broom-so white,—
Such as herself she plucked,—a wreath
I wreath for her tonight:

Flowers of the sunshine & the fells
Where we together roved,
And one — the Eye of day — that spells
The name of my beloved ;

For she was open as the air
Pure as the blue of heaven,
And truer love — or pearl so rare.
To man was never given !

A.J.E.

Fig. 30   Poem written by Arthur Evans in 1893 after the death of his wife Margaret.
(Ashmolean Museum).

The Cretan Thread

Evans was drawn to Crete by his search for an early writing system. He found it hard to believe that the great prehistoric sites, such as Mycenae, recently revealed by Heinrich Schliemann, had been inhabited by an illiterate people. In *Scripta Minoa* vol. I (1909) he wrote: '... in the midst of this brilliant picture of early Aegean civilization there was one notable lacuna. No evidence of the existence of an indigenous system of writing was as yet forthcoming... Was this great early civilization, then, altogether dumb?' As early as 1889 he searched for clues and found evidence—pictographic and linear signs engraved on sealstones, and he read A. Milchhoefer's suggestion in *Die Anfänge der Kunst* (1883) that the principal source of such stones should be sought in Crete. This provenance was confirmed in 1893 when Evans and his young Oxford friend, J.L. Myres, found similar seals, said to be from Crete, in antique shops in Athens. The same year Myres travelled to the Island, and bought some 'hieroglyphic' sealstones, and gave them to the Ashmolean. Evans's appetite was whetted.

Crete had already enthralled many British travellers in the nineteenth century, notably Robert Pashley, who published *Travels in Crete* in 1837, and T.A.B. Spratt, who wrote *Travels and Researches in Crete* in 1865, both recording much of archaeological interest. Evans was doubtless familiar with these publications and almost certainly knew Stillman's report on Crete published in 1881 (Stillman had advised him on Balkan affairs). Signs on stone blocks visible at Knossos, illustrated by Stillman, probably attracted Evans's attention with their similarity to the signs he had noted on seals. In particular, discussions in 1892 with Federico Halbherr, an epigraphist foremost in Cretan scholarship, must have given him a first hand account of the Island's antiquities.

Evans decided to visit Crete to accumulate further evidence for a writing system and to locate ancient sites, particularly those belonging to the Bronze Age period. At the same time he hoped to acquire objects for his own collection and for the Ashmolean, since export was possible before the stringent Antiquities Law of 1899.

This decision to visit Crete was strengthened by Myres's return from the Island bringing fresh information on the antiquities. Myres was chiefly absorbed with Knossos, especially the hilltop Kephala, where the existence of a prehistoric palace had long been known. He had been shown the site by Minos Kalokairinos, a merchant from Heraklion, who had dug in various areas on the Kephala. Some finds from Kalokairinos' excavations were sketched by Myres; others, such as giant pithoi or storage jars, had been dispersed, one being sent to the British Museum.

Myres returned to Oxford intent on excavating at Knossos. But he was dissuaded by both Halbherr and Dr. Hazzidakis, the President of the Heraklion Syllogos; the Cretans rightly feared the depredations of the Turks as many antiquities had already been shipped to Constantinople. The Syllogos was an educational society which collected and preserved the Island's antiquities, and its museum, already of considerable importance, was to become the nucleus of the Heraklion Archaeological Museum.

Despite the failure of Myres's plans, his account of Knossos fired Evans's curiosity. It confirmed the site's importance and the potential for excavation. Evans was not deterred by Myres's withdrawal: his sights were firmly fixed on the Kephala. His own subsequent visit to Knossos increased his determination to excavate, and he was prepared to wait until the political situation was resolved.

Cretan politics

In 1878, at the time Evans was reporting from the Balkans for the *Manchester Guardian*, a major insurrection took place in Crete. The revolt was put down but the Sultan, under international pressure, was forced to restore some earlier concessions. The Halepa Pact was drawn up and heralded, for a short time, a more stable period. The breathing space allowed Minos Kalokairinos to excavate at Knossos, but his investigations were soon stopped. Further outbreaks of violence occurred. Most insurrections entailed appalling losses on both sides. After their suppression concessions were granted by the Porte, only to be reneged on shortly after.

By the last decade of the nineteenth century, the time of Evans's travels, Crete, one of the last outposts of the decadent Ottoman Empire, had reached a critical stage in her history. It could only be a matter of time before the Turks were ousted and the Cretans gained either autonomy or union with Greece. Inevitably Evans became interested in Cretan politics, supporting the Christian Cretans just as he had espoused the cause of the oppressed Christians in the Balkans.

Evans saw the results of the uprisings as he travelled round the island; once-prosperous villages were reduced to burnt out shells, their surrounding olive and carob trees hacked down. Although the whole Island was involved in the revolts, the most rebellious area was Western Crete. Sphakia in particular was a wild, isolated area—Evans avoided it, discouraged by its apparent lack of archaeological interest and doubtless warned by Myres of its dangers.

The first visit to Crete

Evans wrote to Fortnum in November 1893, 'I am getting very restless and want a good run! Nothing will content me but to go round by Sicily to Crete. My own house is going on quite smoothly and there will be an interval of about two months during which I can do nothing either there or in the new Ashmolean whereas later there will be any amount to do.' In Joan Evans's book *Time and Chance*, she writes of her half-brother, 'Time and Chance were now to guide him to a land that for the rest of his life was to be the kingdom of his mind.'

On 14th March 1894 Evans embarked 'on that uncertain element', and sailed for Crete from Athens. He suffered horribly from seasickness and was relieved, after a bad twenty-four hour crossing, when his boat anchored off Candia (Heraklion) and he was rowed ashore. He planned to stay a fortnight, but was captivated as soon as he landed—he stayed on the Island about six weeks. For him travelling through the Cretan countryside was an adventure impossible to hurry—there was so much to discover (map 3). He was enchanted by the mountain ranges of Ida and Dikte, the profusion of wild flowers (colour pl. A), and by views of the White Mountains and the 'wine-dark sea'. Evans was soon to realise that many sites which he saw and some of the objects he collected were earlier than 'Mycenaean', although he continued to use this term. Evidence of a civilization was emerging which he was later to name 'Minoan'.

In Heraklion Evans explored the Venetian ramparts—never had he 'seen such huge fortifications' (fig. 31)—and admired the fountain built in 1628 by the governor, Francesco Morosini (fig. 32). He worked in the Museum and visited dealers, buying several sealstones and a gold ring (colour pl. D). This ring was said to come from Knossos; a scene at an outdoor shrine was engraved on its bezel.

Fig. 31 The ramparts at Candia (Heraklion). (Photograph by N. Heaton, Ashmolean Museum).

Fig. 32   The Morosini fountain, once surmounted by a statue of Neptune. (Photograph by R. Behhaeden, Ashmolean Museum).

Evans was impatient to visit Knossos, and on 19th March, less than a week after his arrival, he went to see the Kephala, 'brilliant with purple white and pinkish anemones and blue iris' (colour pl. A). On a second visit he was accompanied by Minos Kalokairinos who pointed out the areas excavated in 1878—79. At Makryteichos, near Knossos, Evans bought a small fragment of a stone *rhyton* or conical jar, decorated with a cult scene: an open air sanctuary, with two men, a fig-tree and an altar crowned with what he later recognised as bull's horns, the so-called horns of consecration. He also bought a seal engraved with a butterfly; these objects he illustrated in his *Travel Diary* (fig. 33). Evans was determined to excavate the Kephala for himself. He decided to try and purchase the land, held by several Turkish owners, and discussed the possibility with Dr Hazzidakis. Dr Hazzidakis seems to have come to some agreement with Evans about excavation, and aided him in his protracted negotiations to buy the site. He 'poopoohed' an earlier claim by a young archaeologist, André Joubin, acting for the French School at Athens. Joubin had put himself beyond the pale, as far as the Cretans were concerned, by co-operating with the Turks and cataloguing the sculpture in the Imperial Museums in Constantinople for their director, Hamdi Bey.

Leaving Heraklion on 23rd March, Evans set out on his travels with a muleteer and three mules. He rode west, perched uncomfortably on a wooden pack saddle, and reached Rethymnon the following day. At Rethymnon he hired a new muleteer, Alevisos Papalexis, introduced to him by Halbherr. Alevisos was to prove an invaluable guide: he had travelled round the island with Joubin, and later with the Italians; he knew the whereabouts of many sites, how to drive a hard bargain and, an important point with Evans, how to cook! He was later to become an overseer on the Knossos excavation until finally he fell from grace.

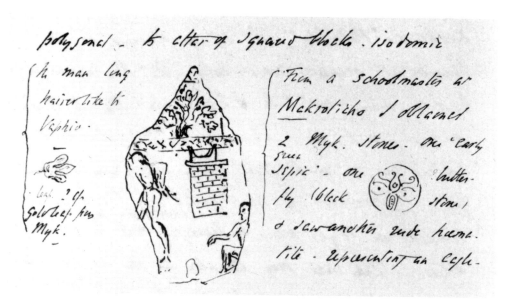

Fig. 33 From Evans's *Travel Diary*, March 19—20, 1894. Serpentine relief rhyton fragment. From Gypsades. Bought at Makryteichos. Late Minoan I, Ht.0.084, Ashmolean no. AE.1247; Lentoid seal, butterfly. Late Minoan. Ashmolean no. 1938.968 (Notebook C, Ashmolean Museum).

In Rethymnon Evans purchased bronze objects from a cave dedicated to the cult of Hermes Kranaios, amongst which was an imported Late Bronze Age statuette of a Syrian god (fig. 34). He also saw material said to have come from the cave in the Museum of the Syllogos. This cave was one of a series near the village of Patsos, which, in 1899, Evans was the first archaeologist to visit.

Fig. 34 Bronze statuette of a Syrian god from the Cave of Hermes Kranaios. Late Bronze Age. Ht.0.153, Ashmolean no. 1894.140=AE.13

On 27th March, Evans and Alevisos rode out from Rethymnon to the Monastery of Arkadi. Evans describes how in 1866 the monastery 'was almost destroyed by the Turks and the scene of an indiscriminate massacre of 550 men, women and children. When all was lost the Hegoumen [Abbot] Gabriel himself fired the magazine.' Evans continues, 'His [Gabriel's] scholar of the same name is the present Hegoumen who received me most hospitably. A jovial man on whom the lenten fasting sits uneasily. He said that before the catastrophe there were 60 monks here; there are now 20, only one of the original brotherhood escaped the massacre, cutting his way out through the Turks.' The peaceful scene in a watercolour by Edward Lear (colour pl. B), contrasts with the violent portrayal of the siege in the *Illustrated London News* (November, 1866) (fig. 15).

The travellers made their way by rugged paths to the Monastery of Asomatos, now a School of Agriculture. Here they met Eumenios, the Bishop of Lambis and Sphakia. Evans found him 'very intelligent' and learnt that he was the best of all Cretan bishops. He gave 'valuable information about antiquities with which this district of Amari swarms.' The Bishop also told Evans how twenty years ago Cretan Moslems had been in the majority, but were now in the minority: 'Very fanatical. No friendship with them possible. Would like to exterminate all Christians.' Six years later Evans was to employ both Christian and Moslem Cretans at Knossos as a contribution to bridging the religious divide.

The weather was bad when Evans left the monastery: 'Wind tremendous, several times almost blown off the horse, and the horse repeatedly blown off the track!' Continuing down the Amari valley Evans was put up in the village of

Fig. 35   The house built by Robert Hay for Kalitza. (Photograph by Author).

Apodoulou by the local priest, of whom he wrote, 'He was old and lame, and his lair was near the fire in a little earth-floored room, where as I sat sheep walked in and out, and now and then an intrusive pig; while an unexpected coney-kin came out between my legs and I found that there was a whole litter of rabbits under his reverence's berth.' The priest was a kinsman of Kalitza Psarakis, daughter of the Chief Magistrate of Apodoulou, who had been abducted and taken to Egypt for the harem. Robert Hay, a Scottish Egyptologist, bought her in the market at Alexandria in 1824 and married her in Malta four years later. Evans was shown a large house in the village which had survived the devastation of 1866. It had been built by Hay for his wife when the couple visited Crete. Above the window the initials KH can still be seen (fig. 35). His next destination was the Kamares Cave (fig. 36).

Fig. 36   The Kamares Cave during excavation for the British School in 1913.
(Ashmolean Museum).

In the Museum in Heraklion Evans had seen sherds of pottery from the Cave, decorated with white, orange and red motifs on a black ground. Some had been drawn by Myres in 1893, who recognised their early date—Kamares Ware pottery dates to the Middle Minoan period. When they reached Kamares, Evans and Alevisos were told that they would be unable to climb up to the Cave as it was blocked with snow. Instead they went back on their tracks to investigate a cemetery composed of several tombs, known as tis Kaïmenis to Sopato—today under vines. Evans 'procured' a bronze knife, found in one of the tombs, from the owner of the land (fig. 37).

Fig. 37 Bronze knife, from a cemetery near Kamares. Late Minoan, L.0.265, Ashmolean no. AE.63

Evans searched in vain for the location of the cemetery of Ayios Onouphrios, which he knew to be near Phaistos. It was said to be the provenance of many objects in the museum in Heraklion—objects which he drew and later published. He also believed the cemetery to be the source of a Middle Minoan shell head (fig. 38) which he had acquired in Heraklion. He noted nothing of interest at Phaistos, where Halbherr was to begin excavating a palace in 1900.

Evans was disappointed when he reached Gortyn. Federico Halbherr, whom he had hoped would show him the Great Inscription, was away on one of his many exploratory forays. The Inscription set out the laws of the city—written in Doric dialect. It dates from the end of the 6th to the beginning of the 5th century B.C. Evans saw, 'everywhere the signs of a great Roman city': the remains of many public buildings, temples and theatres covered a wide area. Architectural fragments littered the fields—some had been used in building the village of Ayii Deka. Excavation continues today on the site and surrounding area.

From Gortyn he travelled east, on a course parallel to the south coast, noting sites and buying objects in the villages. Eventually he reached Myrtos,

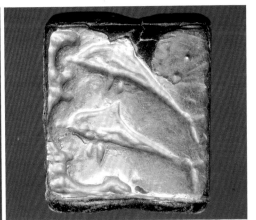

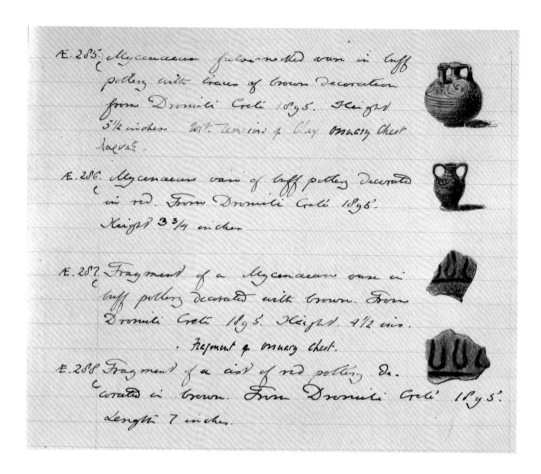

AE.285. Mycenaean false-necked vase in buff pottery with traces of brown decoration from Dromili Crete 1895. Height 5½ inches. Wt. Remains of clay ossuary chest λαρναξ.

AE.286. Mycenaean vase of buff pottery decorated in red. From Dromili Crete 1896. Height 3¾ inches

AE.287. Fragment of a Mycenaean vase in buff pottery decorated with brown. From Dromili Crete 1895. Height. 4½ ins.
. Fragment of ossuary chest.

AE.288 Fragment of a cist of red pottery De. corated in brown. From Dromili Crete 1895. Length 7 inches.

Colour pl. D **Gold ring, Late Minoan. L.0.022. Ashmolean no. 1938.1127.**
(previous page)

Seal, Middle Minoan.
L.0.016. Ashmolean no. 1938.963.

Church of the Holy Apostles, Adromyloi. (Photograph by Author).

Colour pl. E **From Ashmolean Museum register illustrating Late Minoan material from Adromyloi. Ashmolean nos. AE.285—288.**

where he learnt of Roman tombs. British excavations in the 1960s and 1970s have in fact revealed two important Minoan sites in the area: an Early Minoan village at Myrtos-Phournou Koriphi, and Myrtos-Pyrgos, a long-lived settlement where there was a large, grand house in the Late Minoan period.

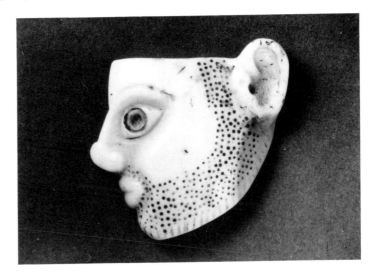

Fig. 38 Shell head. Said to be from Ayios Onouphrios. Middle Minoan, Ht.0.037, Ashmolean no. 1938.537

When he reached Hierapetra Evans was dismayed by this once great city: 'How are the mighty fallen! Hierapytna once sovereign of this part of Crete is now a miserable townlet in the last stage of dilapidation and deadrot.' He noted the time-wasting practice of the villagers who pretended to have valuable objects to show him: 'E.g. in the morning a silversmith induced me to go to his house under the pretence that he had a lot of good silver coins. When I got there he bought out—a Roman lamp of the usual worthless kind. Where were the coins? Oh he had no coins!' Passing through Makryialos—now a small resort, where both Roman and Minoan remains have recently been excavated, Evans turned north, travelling through Lithines to reach nearby Adromyloi, a small village on a prominent rocky spur. He admired the frescoes in its little church, dedicated to the Holy Apostles (colour pl. D). He heard of larnax burials and obtained some small vases (colour pl. E). As always he was on the look out for sealstones, or *galopetres* (milkstones). These had become highly valued, superstitiously worn by nursing mothers, and as such had survived in considerable numbers. 'When not wanted the milkstones are worn on the back "so as not to draw the milk out".'

Evans had been told about Praisos by Halbherr who had first excavated there in 1884, when he found important inscriptions of the 6th, 5th and 4th centuries B.C. He found the Hellenic town was spread over three acropoli, and was the source of many terracotta figurines.

Still travelling east, Evans 'descended into the lovely valley of Epano Zakro, a very oasis, with murmuring millstreams, olives, carobs, figs and rich vegetation of all kinds, peach and apple blossom, poplars in pale spring green, tall cypresses standing out against the grey background of limestone crags.' Near Epano Zakro he explored the site of Athropolithous and bought terracotta animal and human figurines (fig. 39) said to be from a rock shelter. On his plan

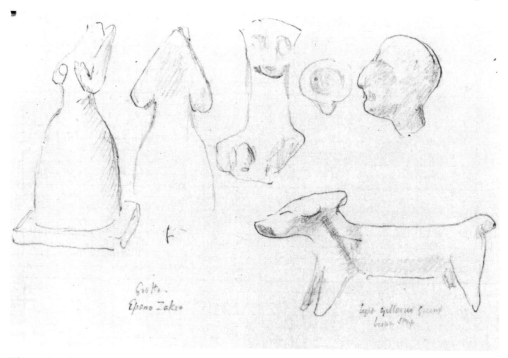

Fig. 39 From Evans's *Travel Diary*; drawings of terracotta figurines from **Athropolithous. Middle to Late Minoan. Ashmolean Museum nos. AE.106—7, 109—110.** (Notebook C, Ashmolean Museum).

(fig. 40) he sketched a large building with thick walls, probably the remains of a Late Minoan villa, known as *tou Koukou to Kephali*—excavated in the 1960s.

Reaching the coast Evans heard of ancient remains on the plain at Palaikastro and rode out to see them. Excavations by R.C. Bosanquet in 1901

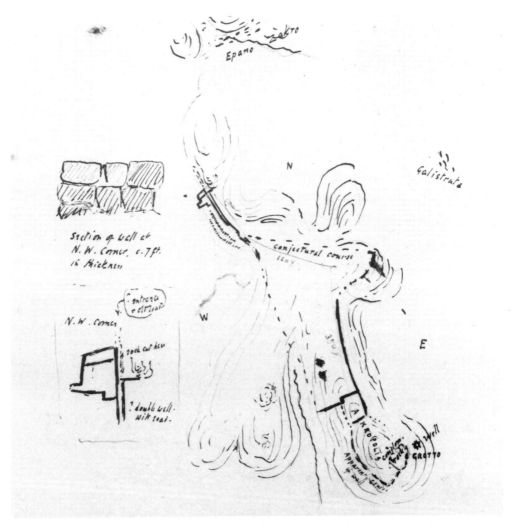

Fig. 40   From Evans's *Travel Diary*; plan of the area of Athropolithous. (Notebook C, Ashmolean Museum).

were to reveal a long-lived Minoan town, laid out carefully with blocks of houses and paved streets. Recent excavations have unearthed further areas of the mainly Late Minoan town—an important ivory male figure has been found. From the plain Evans climbed up the hill of Kastri (now known to have been occupied by settlements dating to the Early and Late Bronze Age), commenting, 'The Paleokastro itself is an isolated limestone hill about hour from the village rising abruptly above the plain on one side and the sea on the other.' In the village he obtained a steatite seal, engraved with a pair of dolphins—its thin gold covering is only partially preserved (colour pl. D). From this he deduced that other stone relief ware, such as the vase fragment (fig. 33), may once have been covered with gold leaf.

Leaving Palaikastro Evans rode along the sandy beach and struck west across the plain, seamed by gullies and swept by the wind, emerging at the Monastery of Toplou, one of the foremost monasteries in Crete: it was 'made for defence with loophole like windows and high surrounding walls.' The monastery had a small cannon—the Turkish word for which may have given the monastery its name. Inside, on the façade of the church, is a Madonna in relief and several inscriptions. Evans thought it worth noting that the Abbot was entertaining two Moslem travellers; at this time in East Crete, Moslem and Christian in the countryside got on tolerably well. Animosity, however, was far more prevalent in the towns.

Evans also visited the little port of Sitia, which had been sacked by Barbarossa in 1538 and abandoned a century later: Evans found that it had been rebuilt and was becoming an important economic centre. He made an excursion to Piskokephalo, about two kilometres south of Sitia, where he saw walling, probably belonging to a Late Minoan villa, on the site now known as Manaris, which was excavated in the 1950s.

He left Sitia on 13th April and travelled through the villages of Skopi and Paraspori to Rhokaka (Roukaka, now called Chrysopigi): 'From Rhokaka ascended a wild limestone gorge overlooked by the heights of the Affendi Vounou range, the lower parts bright with yellow oxalis and higher up among the rocks many tall yellow arums [colour pl. A]. From the top of the pass (1hr) a beautiful view opens of the blue waters of the bay of Mirabello and the snow clad heights of Dikte beyond.' Half an hour from the pass Evans came to the tiny village of Avgo, where massive walling (fig. 41) still stands beside its little church dedicated to the Ayia Panagia. Evans believed this walling to have been part of a small stronghold once guarding the pass. However, Miss Harriet Ann Boyd, the intrepid young American archaeologist who excavated at Avgo in 1901, concluded that the walls were part of a 'megalithic homestead'.

Fig. 41 Walling at Avgo. (Photograph by S. Townsend).

Eventually Evans reached Kritsa—'the largest village in Crete...the starting point for the ruined town of Goulas [Lato] about half an hour's ride to the N.W.' Lato occupies a spectacular position overshadowed by mountains, with views to the north of the bay of Mirabello. Evans was deeply impressed by the massive remains of the large town (colour pl. F), whose public buildings (fig. 42) and houses were built over two hills and the saddle between. He was convinced that Lato was a prehistoric city, comparing the entrance (colour pl. F) to the Lion Gate at Mycenae. He retained his belief even after French excavations (1899—1900) had shown that the remains were mainly Hellenistic. Halbherr had also considered the remains prehistoric and had once cherished the hope that Schliemann might excavate there. An ancient road led from Lato towards Ayios Nikolaos, probably the ancient port of the city. The present large resort was only a small port when Evans visited it. From Ayios Nikolaos he made the short journey to Elunda, where he saw the foundations of ancient buildings in the shallow waters, and remains of walling on the isthmus. He noted Spinalonga (fig. 43), which in 1903 became a leper colony. Lepers were common in Crete and their villages outside the city gates were a sad sight.

Fig. 42   Goulas (Lato). (Ashmolean Museum).

Evans travelled swiftly west to Heraklion where he discussed the purchase of part of the Kephala with Hazzidakis, who agreed to act on his behalf. Before leaving for Oxford Evans wrote a letter to the *Athenaeum* (no. 3478), 'A Mycenaean System of Writing'. Once back in England he was soon busy supervising the transfer of objects from the Ashmolean in Broad Street to their new home. But his thoughts were in Crete, and he made plans to return there the following year.

Fig. 43   View of Spinalonga. (Photograph by R. Behhaeden, Ashmolean Museum).

In 1895 Evans returned to Crete with Myres (map 4), and visited the Lasithi region, an area new to Evans. On their way they stayed the night near the large Roman site of Lyttos, still not fully investigated. Then they climbed up to the 'Tomb of Tsouli'— a pass named, according to folklore, after a Turk called Tsouli. He had made the women of Lasithi dance before him; their menfolk exacted a terrible retribution for this insult, waylaying and killing him at the pass, before throwing his headless body down a cleft; his head was placed in his saddle-bag and his mule returned home with its terrible burden. From the pass the travellers dropped down to the Lasithi plain and reached the village of Psychro (fig. 44, colour pl. J). Evans had bought in 1894 Late Minoan votive bronze

Fig. 44   The village of Psychro, Lasithi. The dark entrance of the cave can be seen on the slope to the right above the village. (Ashmolean Museum).

animal and human figurines (fig. 45), said to have been discovered in a sacred cave above the village—thought by many to be the legendary birth place of Zeus. Myres and Evans clambered down into the dank interior to investigate. They found,'It being the holiday-time of the Greek Easter, a large part of the male inhabitants of the village (fig. 46) were engaged in grubbing in the interstices of the boulders. The huge masses of fallen rock with which almost the whole of the

Fig. 45 Bronze figurines from Psychro cave. Duck: Middle Minoan III—Late Minoan, L.0.05, Ashmolean no. 1894.135=AE.34

Woman: Late Minoan, Ht.0.078, Ashmolean no. 1894.131=AE.22

vast entrance hall of the Cave is strewn, preclude anything like systematic excavation on a large scale within the Cave except at enormous expense.' The Cave, an important cult centre from Middle Minoan times, was excavated in

Fig. 46   The villagers of Psychro posed at the entrance to the Cave. (Photograph by Myres 1895, Ashmolean Museum).

1900 by D.G. Hogarth, Director of the British School at Athens (fig. 47), who used dynamite to shift the fallen rock.

Fig. 47   The Psychro Cave 1900, D.G. Hogarth the excavator. In the foreground Gregori Antoniou, who later became Evans's foreman at Knossos. (Ashmolean Museum)

At the south-east corner of the plain, near Ayios Konstantinos, Evans and Myres climbed up a zigzag track, beyond the church of Ayia Pelagia. Evans was convinced the path dated to 'Mycenaean' times. The travellers crossed the Katharo plain and began the descent to Kritsa. On the way down they found the remains of buildings which they interpreted as 'forts'. When they returned home they wrote an article for the *Academy* (June 1, 1895 no. 1204), entitled 'A Mycenaean Military Road'. The structures they saw have still not been investigated. Bronze Age sherds have been found at many, but until the buildings have been examined little can be said about their date or function. Although some may have belonged to upland hamlets, one, in a spectacular position, could have been a 'fort'. It has an entrance, strong walls, and a watch-tower (figs. 48—50, colour pl. G). Evans called it the 'Kitten's Cistern', but the actual Kitten's Cistern—a site with traces of walling, is further down, off the road to Kritsa, and the 'fort' should more properly be called Akhladies.

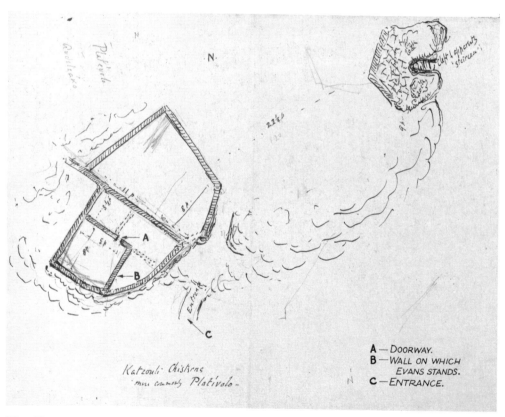

Fig. 48 **Evans's plan of Akhladies.** (Loose sheet T, Ashmolean Museum).

Fig. 49 Evans wearing 'Indian helmet' standing on a wall at Akhladies. (Photograph by Myres 1895, Ashmolean Museum).

Fig. 50   Akhladies. 'Watchtower' from the East. (Photograph by S. Hood, 1948).

From Kritsa Evans took Myres to Goulas (Lato). They spent much time mapping (fig. 51) and photographing the site, including buildings on the Southern Acropolis (fig. 52, colour pl. G). Evans was more than ever convinced that the structures he saw belonged to the Bronze Age. On their return he published an article, 'Goulas: the City of Zeus', in the *Annual of the British School at Athens* (1895—96).

Colour pl. F **Lato (Goulas). North Acropolis.** (Photograph by Author).

Lato. Entrance to the town. (Photograph by Author).

Colour pl. G   **Wall at Akhladies (cf. fig. 49), doorway to right.**
(Photograph by Author).

Lato. Structure on the South Acropolis. (cf. fig. 52).
(Photograph by Author).

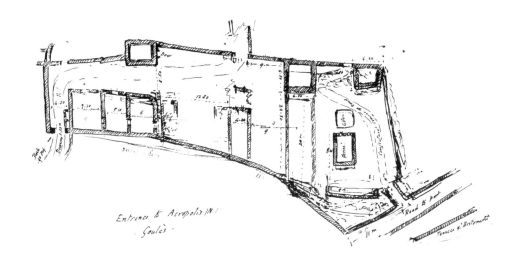

Entrance to Acropolis (N)
Goulas

Fig. 51 Lato. Evans's plan of the entrance to North Acropolis. (Loose sheet T, Ashmolean Museum).

Fig. 52 Lato. Structure on the South Acropolis, Lato. (Photograph by Myres, 1895, Ashmolean Museum).

Explorations in Eastern Crete

In 1896 Evans again visited Crete (map 5), and wrote of his travels in the *Academy* (June 1, 11, July 4 and 7). He revisited the Psychro Cave, where a youth had found a 'broken stone "with writing"'. Naturally Evans lost no time in procuring what proved to be a stone offering table with an inscription (fig. 53). The script which he was later to call Linear A was in use in the late Middle to early Late Minoan period and has still not been deciphered.

He investigated the north side of the Lasithi plain, exploring the site of Ayios Georgios Papoura, before climbing up to Karphi (the 'nail') (colour pl. J). The peak is visible from far away, and a Middle Minoan sanctuary is now known to have been situated on the summit. Clambering up the path Evans came across tholos tombs, some of which he excavated. Below the 'nail' remains of buildings were visible on the south-east slope, spread over a saddle between two peaks. This settlement, excavated by J.D.S. Pendlebury from 1937 to 39, was inhabited

Fig. 53 Fragment of stone offering table, inscribed in Linear A. Middle Minoan, W.0.196, Ashmolean no. AE.1

from the end of the Bronze Age for about 150 years. Evans obtained a little terracotta animal figurine with traces of paint—black spots—said to come from Karphi (fig. 54).

Fig. 54 Terracotta animal figurine, decorated with black spots. Late Minoan, L.0.051, Ashmolean no. 1938.504

Leaving Karphi Evans climbed up a steep, difficult path. He wrote: 'At a spot called Omales ... on a northern spur of Mount Selena, I heard of other ancient ruins...In a wilderness of rock, beneath an ilex wood, where the Cretan wild-goat is still occasionally seen, was one of the most interesting primitive settlements that it has ever been my fortune to explore. It might be described as a "town of castles". The whole consists of a group of "Cyclopean" strongholds, all within hail of one another, each of which, built on its own rock-knoll, with its walled enclosure approached by a fortified ramp, and its inner passages and divisions, might be described as an akropolis in miniature.' Evans sketched plans of two, Ellenika (fig. 55—56, see also fig. 57, colour pl. H), and the 'Mother' fort, known as Monasteraki (figs. 58a—b, see also colour pl. H). Later, after excavating at Knossos, which had been undefended, apparently, and whose frescoes depicted a peaceful, idyllic life, Evans came to believe in a '*pax minoica*' and changed his mind about the function of the structures at Omales, describing them as 'Megalithic houses'. Although Bronze Age sherds have been found on the site, the date of these uninvestigated buildings is unclear.

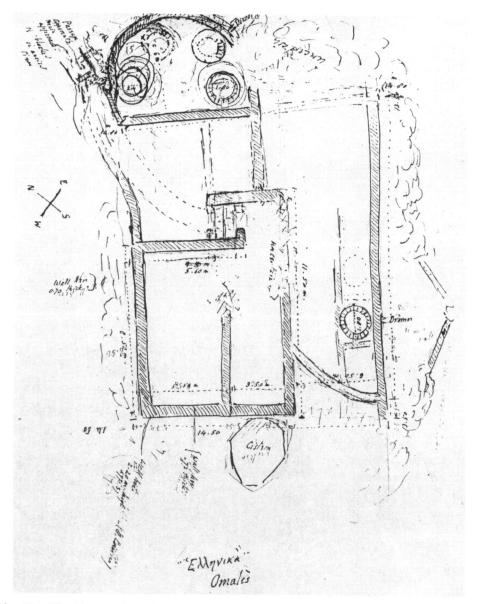

Fig. 55   The Town of Castles, Omales plain: Evans's plan of 'Ellenika'. (Loose sheet T, Ashmolean Museum).

Fig. 56 The Town of Castles, 'Ellenika', N. and W. walls. Drawing by Evans. (Loose sheet T, Ashmolean Museum).

Fig. 57 The Town of Castles, 'Ellenika' W. wall. (Photograph by S. Hood).

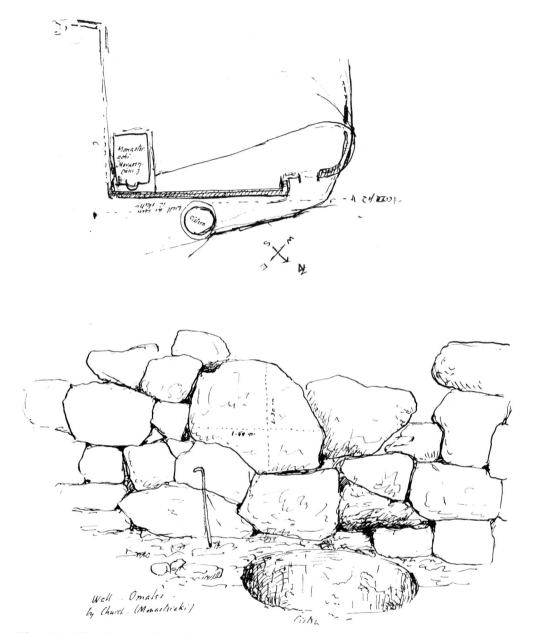

Fig. 58 The Town of Castles, plan of 'Monasteraki', and elevation of 'Wall by Church'. Drawings by Evans. (Loose sheets T, Ashmolean Museum).

Evans once again followed the 'Mycenaean Military Way' and revisited Lato. Travelling east along the north coast he passed Gournia. What he saw here remains enigmatic. Harriet Ann Boyd, the excavator, certainly believed she was the first archaeologist to discover this important Minoan town, but at the same time chides Evans for not having read to her his special notes about Gournia.

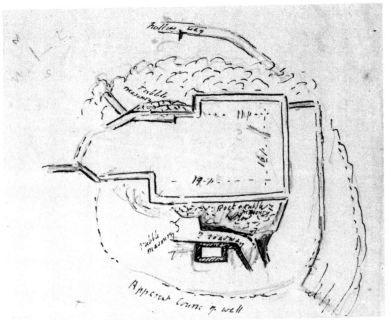

Fig. 59 Evans's plan of Sto Daso Sta Limnia. (Loose sheet T, Ashmolean Museum).

In the far east of Crete Evans discovered a series of sites, described by him as 'forts', many of which are being explored as part of a survey of Minoan roads and the buildings they serve. One site, Kheiromandres, has already been excavated by the Greek Archaeological Service (Y. Tzedakis, S. Chryssoulaki, *et al*.). Here Evans drew walling, a round 'watch-tower' and a 'guard station'.

Another site sketched by Evans, Sto Daso sta Limnia, has been explored by C. Davaras. It lies c. 1400 m. west of the village of Khametoulo. Although a farm building has obliterated some walling, parts drawn by Evans can still be identified (figs. 59—60). Evans returned to Athropolithous and found further terracotta figurines said to be from the rock shelter which he had investigated in

NOW MISSING

Fig. 60 Evans's drawing, annotated to show correspondence with extant walling, Sto Daso Sta Limnia. (Photograph by V. Fotou, 1991).

1894. He went on to 'Ayios Stavromenos' which stands on an isolated hill rising from the plain of Katelionas. The site, under the name Stavros, was surveyed by C. Davaras in 1978, who reported walls made of large blocks, and believes that excavation would be of particular interest.

Revisiting Adromyloi, Evans explored the whole area thoroughly and found the site of Ayios Theodoros on a cliff opposite the village (figs. 61—62). The walls Evans drew are still visible and Bronze Age sherds are scattered over a wide area—but again the site has not yet been excavated.

Continuing along the south coast Evans eventually turned north and reached the Turkish village of Ligortino. He had heard that the village schoolmaster had excavated tholos tombs so he was anxious to explore this area.

Colour pl. H **W. and N. walls, Ellenika (cf. figs. 55—57).**
(Photograph by S. Townsend).

Wall and cistern, Monasteraki (cf. fig. 58).
(Photograph by S. Townsend).

Colour pl. J **Karphi, from the south.** (Photograph by S. Townsend).

Looking south across the Lasithi plain. (Photograph by S. Townsend).

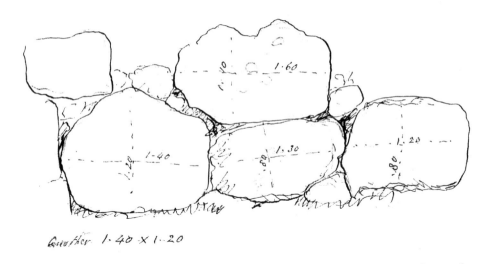

Quoiher 1·40 × 1·20

Fig. 61 Walling at Ayios Theodoros, Adromyloi. Drawing by Evans. (Loose sheet T, Ashmolean Museum).

Fig. 62 Walling at Ayios Theodoros, Adromyloi. (Photograph by V. Fotou, 1991).

Two tombs had yielded many vases (fig. 63), and a painted sarcophagus with a bird on one side. The Moslem inhabitants, described as some of the most fanatical in Crete, would not allow Christians into their houses. Evans, pleading fatigue, asked to rest in a barn where some of the tombs' contents had been stored, and he was thus able to sketch them surreptitiously. Other objects had already been taken to Heraklion for sale, but Evans was able to learn of their position in the tombs from the excavator. Many of the objects from Ligortino were bought by the French traveller Charles Clermont-Ganneau, shipped to Paris and acquired by the Louvre.

Fig. 63   **Plan and contents of 2nd tomb at Ligortino. From Evans's** *Travel Diary.* (Notebook C, Ashmolean Museum).

In 1897 the political situation in Crete was particularly tense and this may have influenced Evans's decision to visit North Africa. He set out early in the year, calling at Sardinia. He was joined by Myres in North Africa on the 3rd of March. They first visited Carthage, where the 'comparison with Venice' struck Evans 'more and more. This too is a city of lagoons.' The two friends travelled to Tripoli with a caravan of seven donkeys, and managed to visit the forbidden interior. There they 'explored the so-called "prehistoric Triliths" and "Great Stone Temples"', finding that these 'were simply great Roman oil establishments, with huge stone presses and all the rest of it.' (fig. 64). Evans returned to Oxford via Malta and Sicily; from Palermo he wrote to Fortnum, 18th April, that he was on his way home, 'safe out of the hands of "Turks, heretics and infidels".'

Fig. 64   Ruins of a Roman oil press, Tarhuna Hills, Tripoli. (Photograph by Evans or Myres, 1897. Ashmolean Museum).

News from Crete

During 1897 Evans kept in touch with Crete, where the tension escalated into fighting. A new dimension was added when Colonel Vassos landed with some 1500 troops claiming the Island in the name of King George of the Hellenes. The intervention of the Greek government had serious implications: not least it encouraged the Christians to arm and indeed massacre many Moslem communities. The Great Powers took charge and called on both Greek and Turkish forces to withdraw from the Island. Order was restored but the Powers retained a strong presence: the French were responsible for Sitia, the British for Heraklion, the Russians for Rethymnon and the Italians for Hierapetra. All four powers were based in the capital, Khania.

Letters from Crete

Evans wrote to Fortnum from Athens, 24th March 1898: 'About to start this evening for Crete...I have seen some of my Cretan friends here and have very bad accounts of most of the island so I don't expect to be able to do much, but there are some tranquil districts...' He travelled to Crete with Myres and Hogarth. In the Balkans he had aided refugees, now he helped deliver barley to the starving Christian villagers. Although he found the Moslems, concentrated in the towns, were hardly better off than their compatriots in the countryside, his sympathies were entirely with the Christian Cretans. Myres and Hogarth departed for Melos leaving Evans to travel east, on a boat carrying relief supplies—he thought it wiser not to ride overland and risk being 'Bashi-Bazouked'. He was determined to revisit the archaeologically rich region of Sitia. Here the aftermath of the previous year's fighting was very apparent and several villages bore the scars. It was all the more distressing to Evans that the Christians had perpetrated many of the atrocities. He gives a graphic account of the scene at Etia, a small Turkish village dominated by a ruined Venetian mansion, probably built by the Dei Mezzo family (fig. 65). The inhabitants of Etia having taken refuge in a mosque, were led out and slaughtered. Evans wrote in *Letters from*

Crete (a privately printed pamphlet publishing his letters to the *Manchester Guardian* in 1898) that no one seemed to have visited the mosque until he 'entered its unhallowed precincts...The clothing of the wretched Moslem villagers, which they gathered together for their flight and left when summoned to their doom still covered the whole floor—bright bits of Oriental covering amidst festering rags, horsehair bags that had contained their scanty stock of food, a green strip from the turban, perhaps, of some descendant of the prophet.'

Fig. 65   Ruin of late 15th century Venetian mansion, Etia. (Photograph probably by Evans, 1898. Ashmolean Museum).

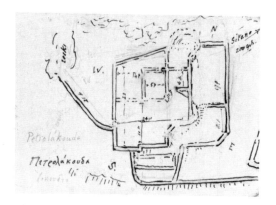

Fig. 66   Evans's plan of a building near Sitanos. (Notebook E, Ashmolean Museum).

Fig. 67   Building near Sitanos. Main S.E. façade, part E. of step back, see Evans's section first wall (fig 66). (Photograph by V. Fotou, 1987).

Returning to Heraklion, Evans fell foul of both the Turkish authorities and the Commander of the British forces, Colonel Chermside. His muleteer Herakles came from Sitia, the scene of Christian atrocities. Herakles had no pass and, although he had helped the French to save many Moslem lives, was arrested by the Turks and kept in a noisome police cell. Evans, having appealed in vain to Colonel Chermside to secure his release, resorted to more subtle methods. He telegraphed the French in Sitia, knowing that Chermside would read the telegram—and not wish to have a diplomatic incident on his hands. Herakles was released; however Evans remained an implacable enemy of the British Commander.

The pamphlet, *Letters from Crete*, contains very little information on Evans's archaeological discoveries, as he intended to publish these separately. His 1898 travel diary is missing, but there are some sketches in a subsidiary notebook. One is of an important building (fig. 66), near the village of Sitanos, previously sketched by an Italian archaeologist, Lucio Mariani. It has recently been investigated by C. Davaras—much of the walling noted by Evans still remains (fig. 67).

Events moved slowly in Crete: Turkish soldiers remained on the Island and a High Commissioner still had not been appointed. All this was to change when, early in September, Moslems rioted in Heraklion and the British Vice-Consul and some British servicemen were killed. It was reported in *The Times*, 10th September, that, 'The Diplomatists uniformly hope that the crisis may extricate the Cretan business from its putrescent stagnations.' By December 1898 Crete was set to gain independence, under the nominal rule of the Sultan, and all but a few Turkish troops had left the Island. The Cretans welcomed Prince George as High Commissioner (fig. 68). His arrival in Khania was greeted with great emotion: many wept openly as he drove through the streets which were garlanded with evergreens. He gave an impassioned speech calling for Christians and Moslems to forget their past animosities, lay down their arms, and work together for the common good.

Evans was greatly encouraged by the political situation: the Island was peaceful and Prince George (fig. 68) was in favour of excavation by foreign schools—if conducted under strict regulations. Evans arrived in Khania (fig. 69, map 6) and found that the French and Italians were already putting in excavation claims. Immediately he arranged to meet the Prince and seek his support to excavate at Knossos on his own behalf, and at further sites on behalf of the British School at Athens.

Leaving Khania he travelled along the north coast, passing through Rethymnon, and went to see the cave near the village of Patsos, the source of several bronzes he had acquired in 1894 (fig. 34). After revisiting the monastery of Arkadi, he left for Eleutherna, 'about 1hr across grassy "polje" with pink

Fig. 68 Prince George. (From, *Illustrated London News,* **February 20, 1897).**

Fig. 69 Khania harbour. (Photograph by N. Heaton, Ashmolean Museum).

tulips (colour pl. A), then over rocky hills and glens with a good deal of verdure—violets, white cyclamen (colour pl. A) and ferns on the banks.' Reaching Eleutherna he walked along a narrow promontory, past a tower 'of massive masonry, of uncertain date, probably late Roman or Byzantine.' Beyond was the acropolis with traces of walls, then, he wrote, 'A small descent on W. side brought us to the openings of two huge underground chambers, hewn out of the living rock.' Evans's guide told him that they were cisterns, and this 'was corroborated by the fact that the walls and pillars had been originally coated by a hard cement.' Following the 'descent' he reached a Hellenistic bridge with triangular arch, spanning a river in the valley below (fig. 70). Excavations on the site were conducted by Humfry Payne for the British School at Athens in 1929; they were resumed for the University of Crete in 1985, and still continue.

Evans returned to Heraklion where he heard from the Prince that he could begin 'trenching' at Knossos if he could prove title to the land, and if he agreed not to export any finds. Any excavation had also to be supervised by a member of the Syllogos. But Evans still could not prove a legal right to the land, although he had bought a quarter of the site back in 1894 and had attempted to force a sale of the remaining three-quarters in the ensuing years.

Hogarth arrived from Athens and, as they were unable to dig at Knossos, he and Evans set off to earmark sites suitable for future British excavation. The first stage of their journey took them to Chersonesos, where they admired the mosaics decorating the remains of a 2nd or 3rd century A.D. pyramidal fountain. They photographed the best preserved side (fig. 71); in the foreground a man

Fig. 70 Eleutherna, the Hellenistic bridge. (Photograph by Evans, 1899. Ashmolean Museum)

gaffs an eel whilst in the centre a second man hauls an octopus into a fishing boat. The mosaics were unprotected and, fearing vandals, Evans urged the 'Chersonesiotes' to erect a fence round the site.

Fig. 71 Mosaic at Chersonesos, one of the sides of the Roman fountain. (Photograph by Author).

Hogarth and Evans retraced earlier journeys. They visited Psychro where, in spite of the difficulties Hogarth could foresee, he decided that he would excavate the cave above the village, perhaps the following year. Then they travelled down 'the Mycenaean Military Way' via Ayios Konstantinos, Akhladies and Kritsa and spent some hours at Lato. Hogarth was rather disappointed with Lato, and correctly identified the walls as belonging to a period later than the Bronze Age. Reaching East Crete they decided that the British School should excavate at Praisos. Then they rode swiftly along the south coast route and eventually returned to Heraklion.

In Heraklion, confident of a favourable outcome to his negotiations for purchasing the land, Evans set about planning the excavation at Knossos. He also discussed future British School excavations with Hogarth. Both were concerned with the new Antiquities Law and how it would affect their work. They also discussed how the excavations were to be financed, and decided to establish a *Cretan Exploration Fund*, which they hoped would provide the necessary money for their enterprises. In the event, comparatively little money was raised from this source and it was fortunate that Evans was a wealthy man, able to spend his money on excavation and restoration.

Evans's discernment and determination were rewarded when, at the end of March, 1900, he began excavating at Knossos. His career up until this point had been distinguished and colourful; he was to go on to achieve a dimension of success that is rare.

Epilogue

When his half-sister Joan decided to call her book on Arthur Evans and his forebears *Time and Chance* (1943) she epitomized his professional life in a phrase. Born of a distinguished family with ample financial resources he was able from an early age to make the most of the many opportunities that came his way. Invariably he was in the right place at the right time. Notably the adventurous travels of his youth, exploring cultures ancient and modern, were a brilliant preparation for his work as a journalist, and his subsequent discoveries in Crete. But the impetus for his career also came from remarkable personal attributes: curiosity, energy and determination combined with an acute eye, a sharp, innovative intellect and a flair for writing. These skills were enhanced rather than diminished by forthright prejudices.

The legacy of Arthur Evans is manifold. He is best known for identifying three Bronze Age writing systems—the hieroglyphic or pictographic script (fig. 72), Linear A (fig. 53) and Linear B — and for his excavations and research at Knossos: the source of immeasurable enrichment to our knowledge of ancient Mediterranean culture. But his contribution before 1900, as this book hopes to have illustrated, must not be underestimated. His writings, published and unpublished, have inspired and informed successive generations of Balkan specialists. Above all students of Crete, which so captivated Evans, have been influenced by his accounts and surveys of sites, many of which still remain to be investigated.

Finally the Ashmolean Museum bears witness to Evans's talent for creative museum administration, his acumen as a collector, as well as to his skills as an archaeologist. Through his acquisitions from Crete, the Ashmolean has become established as an international centre, second only to Heraklion, for the study of Bronze Age Aegean archaeology.

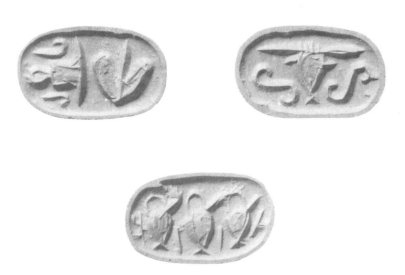

Fig. 72 Impressions of a three-sided seal with hieroglyphic or pictographic signs. Middle Minoan, L.0.02, Ashmolean Museum no. 1938.774

Select Bibliography

Evans, A.J.   'Over the Marches of Civilised Europe', *Fraser's Magazine*, May 1873, vol.7, no.XLI.

"   *Through Bosnia and the Herzegovina on foot, during the Insurrection, August and September 1875, with an historical review of Bosnia* (London, 1876; 2nd ed. revised and enlarged, 1877).

"   *Illyrian Letters: a revised selection of correspondence from the Illyrian provinces of Bosnia, Herzegovina, Montenegro, Albania, Dalmatia, Croatia and Slavonia* (London, 1878).

"   *The Ashmolean Museum as a Home of Archaeology in Oxford. An Inaugural Lecture* (Oxford, 1884).

"   'Antiquarian Researches in Illyricum, I—II and III—IV', *Archaeologia* 48 (1885) 1—105 and 49 (1886) 1—167.

"   *Cretan Pictographs and Prae-Phoenician script; with an account of a sepulchral deposit at Hagios Onuphrios near Phaestos in its relation to primitive Cretan and Aegean culture* (London, 1895).

"   'Explorations in Eastern Crete', *The Academy* (1896) Nos.1258—59, 1261, 1263.

"   'Goulas: the City of Zeus', *Annual of the British School at Athens*, 2 (1895—6) 169—194.

"   *Letters from Crete* (Reprinted from the *Manchester Guardian* of May 24, 25, and June 13 (Oxford, privately printed, 1898).

"   *Further Discoveries of Cretan and Aegean Script, with Libyan and Proto-Egyptian Comparisons* (London, 1898).

"   *The Palace of Minos. A comparative account of the successive stages of the early Cretan Civilization as illustrated by the Discoveries at Knossos*, I—IV (London, 1921—35).

Evans, A.J. and Myres, J.L. 'A Mycenaean Military Road', *The Academy*, 1895) no. 1204.

Evans, J.   *Time and Chance, the Story of Arthur Evans and his Forebears* (London, 1943).

Horwitz, S.L. *The Find of a Lifetime, Sir Arthur Evans and the Discovery of Knossos* (New York and London (1981).

Wilkes, J.J.   'Arthur Evans in the Balkans 1875—81', *Bulletin of the Institute of Archaeology, University of London*, 13 (1976) 25—56.

Maps

Map 1   Sweden and Finland _____ 1871
                   Prepared from Evans's 1873 *Travel Diaries*

Map 2   Boznia and the Herzgovinia _____ 1873
                   Taken from Evans's map in *Through Bosnia*
                   and the Herzegovinia

Map 3   Crete _____ 1894
                   Prepared from Evans's *Travel Diary*

Map 4   Crete _____ 1895
                   Prepared from *The Academy* 1895

Map 5   Crete _____ 1896
                   Prepared from The Academy 1896
                   and Evans's incomplete *Travel Diary*

Map 6   Crete _____ 1898/9
                   Prepared from Evans's incomplete *Travel Diary*
                   and Hogarth's unpublished *Diary*

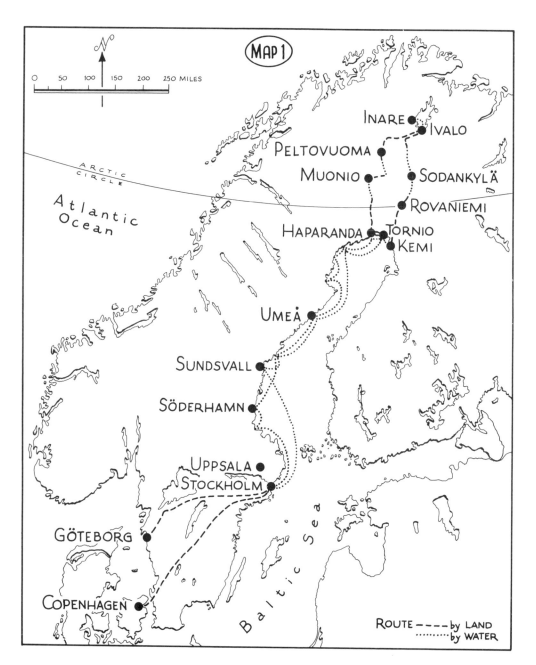

MAP 1

N

0   50   100 150 200 250 MILES

ARCTIC CIRCLE

Atlantic Ocean

INARE
IVALO
PELTOVUOMA
MUONIO
SODANKYLÄ
ROVANIEMI
HAPARANDA
TORNIO
KEMI
UMEÅ
SUNDSVALL
SÖDERHAMN
UPPSALA
STOCKHOLM
GÖTEBORG
COPENHAGEN

Baltic Sea

ROUTE —— by LAND
·········· by WATER

90

AGRAM (ZAGREB)   MAP 2

N

0   10   20   30   40   50 MILES

SIZSEK

CROATIA

KOSTAINICA

BROOD

TESANJ

B O S N I A

SERAJEVO
(SARAJEVO)

A D R I A T I C

D A L M A T I A

MOSTAR

H E R Z E G Ó V I N A

METKOVIĆ

Adriatic

RAGUSA
(DUBROVNIK)

MONTENEGRO

Sea

ROUTE --- by LAND
.... by WATER

91

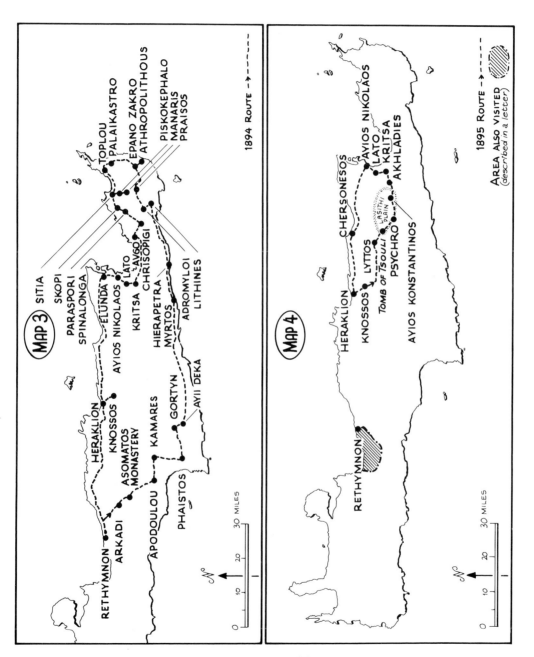

MAP 3

1894 Route - → - - -

SITIA
SKOPI
PARASPORI
SPINALONGA
TOPLOU
PALAIKASTRO
EPANO ZAKRO
ATHROPOLITHOUS
PISKOKEPHALO
MANARIS
PRAISOS
ELUNDA
LATO
AVGO
AYIOS NIKOLAOS
KRITSA
CHRISOPIGI
HIERAPETRA
MYRTOS
ADROMYLOI
LITHINES
HERAKLION
KNOSSOS
ASOMATOS
MONASTERY
KAMARES
GORTYN
AYII DEKA
RETHYMNON
ARKADI
APODOULOU
PHAISTOS

30 MILES
0   10   20

N

MAP 4

1895 Route - → - - -

AREA ALSO VISITED
(described in a letter)

AVIOS NIKOLAOS
LATO
KRITSA
AKHLADIES
CHERSONESOS
LYTTOS
Tomb of Tsouli
LASITHI
PLAIN
PSYCHRO
AYIOS KONSTANTINOS
HERAKLION
KNOSSOS
RETHYMNON

30 MILES
0   10   20

N

92

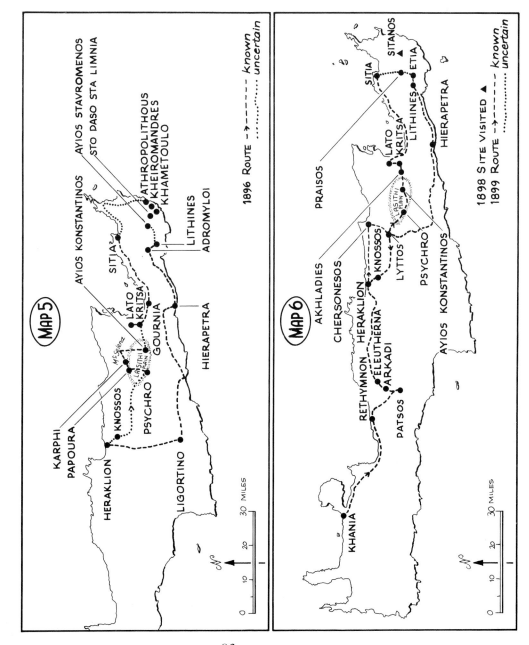

MAP 5

KARPHI
PAPOURA

AYIOS STAVROMENOS
STO DASO STA LIMNIA

ATHROPOLITHOUS
KHEIROMANDRES
KHAMETOULO

LITHINES
ADROMYLOI

AYIOS KONSTANTINOS

SITIA

LATO
KRITSA

GOURNIA

HIERAPETRA

KNOSSOS

PSYCHRO

HERAKLION

LIGORTINO

Mt. Seleña

LASITHI
PLAIN

1896 Route → ----- known
.... uncertain

N

30 MILES
0 10 20

MAP 6

PRAISOS

AKHLADIES

CHERSONESOS

HERAKLION

RETHYMNON
ELEUTHERNA
ARKADI

PATSOS

KHANIA

SITIA

SITANOS

LATO
KRITSA
LITHINES
ETIA

HIERAPETRA

KNOSSOS
LYTTOS

PSYCHRO

AYIOS KONSTANTINOS

LASITHI
PLAIN

1898 Site Visited ▲
1899 Route → ----- known
.... uncertain

N

30 MILES
0 10 20

ASHMOLEAN MUSEUM PUBLICATIONS

Archaeology, History and Classical Studies

Treasures of the Ashmolean

Ancient Egypt

Ancient Greek Terracottas

The Ancient Near-East

The Ancient Romans

The Arundel Marbles

Scythian Treasures in Oxford

Arthur Evans and the Palace of Minos